850

Reasons to Hate
DEMOCRATS

An A to Z Guide to Everything Loathsome

About the Party of Big Government

Barbara Lagowski and Rick Mumma

A BIRCH LANE PRESS BOOK
Published by Carol Publishing Group

A Birch Lane Press Book
Published by Carol Publishing Group
Birch Lane Press is a registered trademark of Carol Communications, Inc.
Editorial, sales and distribution, rights and permissions inquiries should be addressed to
Carol Publishing Group, 120 Enterprise Avenue, Secaucus, NJ 07094.

In Canada: Canadian Manda Group, One Atlantic Avenue, Suite 105, Toronto, Ontario
    M6K 3E7

Carol Publishing Books may be purchased in bulk at special discounts for sales promotion,
fund-raising, or educational purposes. Special editions can be created to specifications. For
details, contact: Special Sales Department, Carol Publishing Group, 120 Enterprise Avenue,
Secaucus, NJ 07094.

Manufactured in the United States of America
10 9 8 7 6 5 4 3 2 1

Library of Congress Cataloging-in-Publication Data
Lagowski, Barbara.
    888 reasons to hate Democrats : an A to Z guide to everything loathsome about the
party of big government / Barbara Lagowski and Rick Mumma.
        p. cm.
    "A Birch Lane Press book."
    ISBN 1-55972-365-3 (pb)
    1. United States—Politics and government—1993 —Humor.
  2. Democratic Party (U.S.)—Humor.   I Mumma, Rick.   II. Title.
E885.L345   1996
324.2736'0207—dc20   96-34151
                                                                        CIP

They condone Bert and Ernie's sexually ambivalent lifestyle.
They have all the files at the FBI . . . and not in the
personnel department. But are there really
888 Reasons to Hate Democrats?

You bet your no-show job and lucrative special entitlements there
are! And this politically-incorrect litany of memorable party lines
("If anyone wants to put a tail on me, go ahead. They'd be very
bored." —Gary Hart), symbols, and slurs resurrects them all just in
time for what promises to be another mud-slinging, mind-numbing
election season.

Remember Hillary's uncanny "beginner's luck"? The party-
wide misconception that the Carter years *weren't* a wash because at
least we all learned to siphon gas? We do. And in this non-federal-
ly funded (and therefore completed in our lifetimes) collection of
separate but equal political foibles past and present, we reveal more
Democrat quirks and curiosities then there are empties in the
Kennedy recycling bin. Including, their liberal standards ("They'll

burn draft cards. They'll burn flags. They'll burn just about anything but fossil fuel"); their double-standards ("They'll give mouth-
to-mouth to a beached whale but they won't allow a good steak to
cross their lips"); their strengths and weaknesses ("They make great
bartenders but lousy husbands"); and their contrbutions to culture
("Thanks to them, you'll never see Stimey on TV again.")

Of course, there are many ugly commonalities that
Republicans and Democrats share. Like law degrees. Embarrassing
relatives. And Martha Stewart. But their most memorable charac-
teristics are like Gennifer Flowers—clearly split among party lines.

Written in brief, biting out-of-context and *always* negative
sound bites (just like your favorite news broadcast!), this collection
is our paean to the political partiers who refuse to accept any military rank lower than Commander-in-Chief . . . who pick up dogs by
their ears and women by worse places than that . . . and who think
Bob Dole is too old to be president—but everyone with permanent
teeth is old enough for Norplant.

Politics . . . the systematic organization of hatreds.
—Henry Adams, *The Education of Henry Adams*

Hell, I never vote *for* anybody, I always vote *against*.
—W. C. Fields

888

Reasons to Hate

DEMOCRATS

1. To them, abortion is a method of birth control.

2. Abscam

3. Abstract "art"

4. They accept themselves just as they are.

5. They moan about the environmental effects of acid rain
   when they ought be worried about the genetic effects
   of those electric Kool-Aid acid tests that seemed like
   such a groovy idea thirty years ago.

6.   The ACLU

7.   ACT-UP

8.   Acupuncture (if it comes from Communist China and undermines American pharmaceutical companies, it's got to be good)

9.   They're addicted to twelve-step recovery programs (but only after any references to God have been expunged)

10.   They believe that adultery can actually strengthen a marriage.

11.   Affirmative action

☆☆☆☆☆☆☆☆☆☆☆☆☆☆☆☆☆☆☆☆☆☆☆☆

12. The AFL-CIO

13. Afrocentric education

14. Agitators

15. Aid for Families with Dependent Children

16. Aid for families without children

17. Aid for children without families

18. The Clintons' use of Air Force One as an extension of Christophe's salon

19. Alan Alda's sensitivity act

20. Woody Allen's family values

21. They allowed the Secret Service to wear gloves when greeting gay activists at the White House. (Anyone who's been to finishing school knows that it is acceptable only for *women* to shake hands while wearing gloves.)

22. Alternative genders

23. Alternative lifestyles

24. Alternative rock (as if regular rock weren't bad enough)

25. Alternative service for those too chicken to fight for their country

26. They're altruistic as long as they're paying their debt to society with somebody else's tax dollars.

27. They prefer the Fifth Amendment to the Second.

28. They only drive American cars if they're running for office.

29. Americans for Democratic Action

30. Carter's amnesty for the draft dodgers in Canada

31. Amy and Chelsea could pick up a few pointers on good grooming from Tricia and Julie.

32. Androgyny

33. They still root for Apple over IBM.

34. Apparatchiks

35. They are "in touch with their female side"—unless they happen to be Democratic women.

36. Arkansas ("I didn't make Arkansas the butt of ridicule. God did."—H. L. Mencken)

37. Artists who demand federal grants to attack the bourgeoisie.

38. They think "Ask what you can do for your country" is just another excuse for higher taxes.

39. Ed Asner

40. Atonal music

41. They attack the middle-class suburban values of the parents who paid their tuition.

42. They prefer backpacks to briefcases.

43. Alec Baldwin

44. Bandannas

45. Bandannas on Irish Setters

46. They want to ban *Huckleberry Finn* from schools because Mark Twain wasn't prescient enough to call Jim an African-American in 1884.

47. They banned school prayer.

48. They gave Marion Barry a second "crack" at the D.C. mayor's office.

49. The Bay of Pigs

50. They beatify self-destructive drug abusers like Jerry, Jimi, and Janis (but go berserk at the thought that George Bush might have taken Halcion).

51. Beatniks

52. David Dinkins's "beautiful mosaic"

53. Beggars who pose as "the Homeless"

54. Be-ins

55. Bell bottoms

56.

57. None of the berets you find in their closets will be green.

58. Berkeley

59. Leonard Bernstein

60. The betrayal of our boys in Vietnam

61. They know how to use a bidet but not a finger bowl.

62. They have more faith in the Big Bang than the Bible.

63. Big city Democratic machines

64. Big cities (except for the financial districts)

65. Big government

66. Bilingual ballots

67. Bilingual education

68. The Billary Administration

69. Billy Beer

70. They accept "Black English" as a legitimate American dialect, but not Greenwich Lockjaw.

71. Black Panthers

72. Black Power

73. They blame America first.

74. They blame "The System" for their own lack of ambition.

75. Bleeding hearts

76. Blonde jokes (and the other forms of politically-correct racism)

77. "Bloom County"

78. Blue collars

79. Blue hair on women who are nowhere near seventy

80. Blue movies

81. Robert Bly

82. They prefer body odor to ozone-depleting deodorant delivery systems.

83. Bohemians

84. Bolsheviks

85. They owned bongs.

86. They owned bongos.

☆☆☆☆☆☆☆☆☆☆☆☆☆☆☆☆☆☆☆☆☆☆☆☆☆

87. They "Borked" the most brilliant jurist nominated to the Supreme Court in this century.

88. They were born with plastic spoons in their mouths.

89. They consider "The Bourgeoisie" an insult rather than an aspiration.

90. Boxes of 16 "flesh-toned" Crayolas for everyone!

91. Jerry Brown's uplinks to extraterretrial consultants

92. Murphy Brown's upscale fictional version of single motherhood

93. Hash brownies

☆☆☆☆☆☆☆☆☆☆☆☆☆☆☆☆☆☆☆☆☆☆☆☆

94. Bubbas

95. Budget deficits

96. Burning bras

97. Burning draft cards

98. Burning flags

99. Burning everything but fossil fuels

100. Cannabis residue (seeds and stems) in the creases of their old double albums

☆☆☆☆☆☆☆☆☆☆☆☆☆☆☆☆☆☆☆☆☆☆

101. Cadillac-driving welfare cheats

102. Campaign promises

103. Capital Gains taxes

104. Card-carrying ACLU members

105. Card-carrying Communists

106. Card-carrying union members

107. Billy Carter

108.

COURTESY: JIMMY CARTER LIBRARY

☆ ☆

109. James "the Ragin' Cajun" Carville

110. They consider Carlos Castaneda a serious philosopher.

111. The rise of casual "dress down" Fridays

112. Cat people

113. A cat *and its litter box* living in the White House

114. When they hear "CDs," and they think of Hootie and the Blowfish rather than Certificates of Deposit.

115. Chappaquidick

116. Cesar Chavez

117. Chicago, 1968

118. The dead Chicago voters who elected JFK in 1960.

119. The Children's Defense Fund

120. They complain about downsizing after *their* unions forced corporations to use more economical Chinese prison labor.

121. They take Christ out of Christmas.

122. Chronic fatigue syndrome

123. Henry Cisneros's philandering eye

124. Connie Chung

125. The only CIA they appreciate is the Culinary Institute of America.

☆ ☆

126. Forcing women on the Citadel

127. Civil (and uncivil) disobedience

128. Civil rights without civil responsibilities

129. They think of themselves as Civil servants, even though *real* servants can be fired.

130. Class action lawsuits

131. Class warfare

132. The Clean Air Act

133. The Clean Water Act

☆☆☆☆☆☆☆☆☆☆☆☆☆☆☆☆☆☆☆☆☆☆☆

134.

135.

136. Clinton's vacillating Bosnia policy

137. Clinton's vacillating China policy

138. Clinton's vacillating Cuban policy

139. Clinton's vacillating marriage vows

140. "Socks" Clinton

141. Clock watchers

142. Little League coaches who don't care whether the game is won or lost

143. They want to be coddled from cradle to grave.

144. Coed bathrooms

145. Coed dormitories

146. Coed soccer

147. Coed military units

148. They want every institution to be coed except for elite women's colleges.

149. They prefer coexistence to victory over Communism.

150. Coffee house poetry

151. Cohabitation without benefit of legal and ecclesiastical sanction

152. They prefer Colt .45 the beverage to Colt .45 the firearm.

153. The only "Combat" they've had any experience with is the ant and roach killer

154. They throw coming-out parties for thirty-year old males who will never breed rather than for females of good breeding in their late teens.

155. Communes

156. They would prefer one hundred Communists in the State Department to one Joe McCarthy in the Senate.

157. They brag about their compost piles.

158. They prefer compassion to competition.

159. Condom ads on television

160. Condom giveaways in grammar schools

161. They condone Bert and Ernie's sexually ambivalent lifestyle.

162. They would rather confess to Jenny Jones than to a priest.

☆☆☆☆☆☆☆☆☆☆☆☆☆☆☆☆☆☆☆☆☆☆☆☆

163. Conscientious objectors, i.e., cowards.

164. Consciousness raising, i.e., the feminazi brainwashing of our wives and mothers

165. Conspiracy nuts

166. They constantly ask what the country can do for them.

167. Hillary's put-down of moms who bake cookies

168. Cornrows (and we don't mean the kind you see in Iowa)

169. The counterculture

170. They prefer creativity to productivity.

171. Criminals' rights

172. R. Crumb

173. Mario "I'm-too-smart-to-condescend-to-being-your-President" Cuomo

174. Cynicism about God and country

175. Martin Luther King Day

176. Take Our Daughters to Work Day

☆☆☆☆☆☆☆☆☆☆☆☆☆☆☆☆☆☆☆☆☆☆☆

177. World AIDS Day

178. Earth Day

179. Any other "Day" that's really just an excuse by anti-capitalist forces to eat into the already declining productivity of the American "worker"

180. They prefer any Day to Doris Day

181. Deadheads

182. Death-bed converts

183. *Deep Throat*, the movie

184. Deep Throat, the turncoat who ratted on Nixon.

185. Defenders of school busing who live in all-white suburbs

186. Defenders of busing who live in the White House and send their daughter to a private school

187. Defense lawyers

188. Deficit spending

189. The deification of Eleanor Roosevelt

190. The deification of Jacqueline Bouvier Kennedy Onassis

☆☆☆☆☆☆☆☆☆☆☆☆☆☆☆☆☆☆☆☆☆☆☆☆

191. The demonization of the equally thin and stylish Nancy Davis Reagan

192. Demagogic appeals to class resentments

193. The denigration of Western culture

194. The Department of Education

195. The Department of Energy

196. The Department of Health and Human Services

197. The Department of Housing and Urban Development

198. The Department of Labor

199. "Dykes on Bikes"

200. They view disability payments for life as state-sponsored Lotto for the working class.

201. Discrimination against straight white males

202. They are even better at dodging questions than dodging the draft.

203. Do-gooders

204. The "do your own thing" philosophy

☆☆☆☆☆☆☆☆☆☆☆☆☆☆☆☆☆☆☆☆☆☆☆

205. They do not have any idea what to do with their hair.

206. They prefer living on the dole to voting for Bob Dole.

207. Phil Donahue

208. Sam Donaldson

209. "Don't ask, don't tell"

210. "Doonesbury"

211. Doves

212. Drag queens

☆☆☆☆☆☆☆☆☆☆☆☆☆☆☆☆☆☆☆☆☆☆☆

213. Dreadlocks

214. Dress code violations

215. They drift through life expecting the middle class to foot the bill for their lifeboat.

216. They drink too much just so they can feel good about recycling the extra bottles.

217. They nominated Michael Dukakis.

218. Some of them *voted* for Michael Dukakis.

219. "Eat the rich" graffiti and T-shirts

220. Their idea of ecumenism includes animists, Satanists, Buddhists, pagans, and Unitarians.

221. They're "an effete corps of impudent snobs who characterize themselves as intellectuals."—Spiro Agnew

222. Effeminacy (except among Democrat women)

223. Eggplant pizza

224. Jocyelyn Elders's feelings about legal drugs and solo sex

225. Electric cars

226. Electric guitars (played by anyone but Lee Atwater)

227. They prefer Ellis Island to Plymouth Rock (but still feel entitled to a free turkey dinner every Thanksgiving).

228. Daniel Ellsburg

229. Embarrassed by American superpower status

230. The Endangered Species Act

231. "Democrats are the enemy of normal Americans."
    —Newt Gingrich

232. Entitlement Programs

233. The jackbooted thugs of the Environmental Protection Agency Environmental

234. The Equal Employment Opportunity Commission's campaign to force Hooters to hire waitpersons with pecs instead of breasts

235. Their only experience with equestrian sports is at the two-dollar betting window.

236. The ERA, which would have had us all using co-ed urinals by now

237. They prefer estrogen to testosterone.

238. They prefer *ET* to *Independence Day.*

239. They prefer ethnic food to meat and potatoes.

240. Even their mothers don't like them: "Sometimes I think to myself, Lillian, you should've stayed a virgin."
—Lillian Carter

241. Everything they need to know about life they learned from *Kung Fu* reruns.

242. They use poverty as an excuse for every evil, from purse snatching to worldwide Communist conspiracies.

243. They're extremists posing as moderates.

244. They think the F word is protected as free speech, just like flag burning.

245. Barney Fa . . . Frank

246. They have faith in the justice system only when the jury is chosen in South Central or the Bronx.

247. Louis Farrakhan

248. They all have FBI files (and not in the personnel department).

249. They "feel your pain."

250. Female condoms

251. Female high-school football players

252. Feminazis

253. Geraldine Ferraro

254. Fifteen-second attack ads

255. They prefer Andy Warhol's fifteen minutes of fame to good, honest work.

256. The 55-mile-per-hour national speed limit

257. "A liberal is a man who leaves the room [or the country] when the fight begins."—Heywood Broun

258. Filibusters against spending cuts

259. They suffer from flashbacks that have nothing to do with the horrors of war.

☆☆☆☆☆☆☆☆☆☆☆☆☆☆☆☆☆☆☆☆☆☆

260. Bill Clinton's Fleetwood Mac revival

261. Flower children

262. Flower power

263. Gennifer Flowers

264. Folk singers

265. "Follow me around. I don't care...If anyone wants to put a tail on me, go ahead. They'd be very bored."
—Gary Hart

266. Jane Fonda's photo-op on a North Vietnamese anti-aircraft gun

267. Food stamps

268. Former presidents who meddle in foreign affairs

269. Former presidents who write silly books with his daughter Amy

270. They only think of Betty Ford as the founder of their favorite spa.

271. Foreign aid

272. Foreign cars on American roads

273. Foreign languages in American schools

274. Their foreign policy would return Alaska to Russia, Louisiana to France, Texas to Mexico, and everything else to the Apaches and Sioux.

275. They forget that they were once fetuses.

276. Vincent Foster's missing files

277. "Republicans believe every day is the Fourth of July, but Democrats believe every day is April fifteenth."
—Ronald Reagan

278. Fragging

279. They once let their "freak flags fly."

☆☆☆☆☆☆☆☆☆☆☆☆☆☆☆☆☆☆☆☆

280. Free association

281. Free breakfasts

282. Free cheese

283. Free clinics

284. Free condoms

285. Freeloaders

286. "Free Huey"

287. Free love

☆ ☆

288. Free lunch programs in inner city schools that keep kids from learning that there is no such thing as a free lunch

289. What the hell is a free-range chicken?

290. Free speech for all (except supporters of Jesse Helms or Newt Gingrich)

291. Free-spending legislators

292. Friends of Bill

293. Frisbee was their only athletic activity in college.

294. Fruitarians

295. The Fruit of Islam

296. Fruits

297. "Elections are about fucking your enemies. Winning is about fucking your friends."—James Carville, 1992

298. Fuel economy stickers

299. Clinton's "funk" is your malaise.

300. They believe the only good fur is a spray-painted fur.

301. Gangsta [sic] rap

☆☆☆☆☆☆☆☆☆☆☆☆☆☆☆☆☆☆☆☆☆☆☆

302. "Gas guzzler" taxes on normal American cars

303. Gays in the military

304. Clinton's attempt to reduce the Gender Gap by appealing to female voters one woman at a time

305. Gender-neutral sports

306. Gender-neutral want ads (Does anybody really want a male secretary?)

307. "Generation X"

308. Generic food packaging

☆☆☆☆☆☆☆☆☆☆☆☆☆☆☆☆☆☆☆☆☆☆☆☆☆

309. JFK Jr.'s "non-partisan" magazine

310. George, the first "Counterculture McGovernick"

311. They prefer Candace Gingrich to Newt

312. Ginseng

313. Dick Gephardt's scary eyebrowless forehead

314. Girls on the Little League diamond

☆☆☆☆☆☆☆☆☆☆☆☆☆☆☆☆☆☆☆☆☆☆☆☆

315. The Global Warming hoax

316. They "Go Ask Alice" for advice on recreational drug consumption.

317. They go ask Amy for advice on nuclear disarmament.

318. They think God is a black, gay, "handi-capable" woman.

319. They think God is dead but Elvis is alive, well, and living at 1600 Pennsylvania Avenue

320. Goddess worship (formerly known as witchcraft)

321. Al Gore's environmental extremism

322. Because Tipper Gore (a preppy woman with a preppy name who had the good taste to attack the music industry) won't admit she's a Republican.

323. They're lousy tippers.

324. Government shutdowns

325. They prefer Grace Slick to Grace Kelly.

326. They see graffiti as an urban art form.

327. Granola

☆☆☆☆☆☆☆☆☆☆☆☆☆☆☆☆☆☆☆☆☆☆

328. They still won't buy grapes.

329. LBJ's Great Society

330. *The Greening of America*

331. Greenpeace

332. The Greens

333. Greenwich Village

334. Gridlock

335. Grunge rock

336. Lani Guinier, the quota queen

337. Hackers clogging up the information superhighway

338. Hackers clogging up the public golf courses

339. They have kicked more hacky sacks than footballs.

340. Haight-Ashbury

341. They want a handout, not a hand up.

342. They measure happiness in orgasms rather than dollars.

☆☆☆☆☆☆☆☆☆☆☆☆☆☆☆☆☆☆☆☆☆☆☆

343. Gary Hart

344. They have made love in the back of a Volkswagen minibus.

345. They have slept two to a sleeping bag with a member of the opposite sex.

346. They have slept two to a sleeping bag with a member of the same sex.

347. They have to keep their Aqua Velva locked in the liquor cabinet.

348. Bill and Hillary's Health Care "crisis"

349. Health nuts

350. Health food stores

351. *Heather Has Two Mommies*

352. *Heather Has Two Mommies and Her Father is a Turkey Baster*

353. Hedonists

354. They don't believe that the road to Hell is paved with good intentions (because they're on it).

355. Hemp extremists

☆ ☆

356. Herbal teas

357. "Herstory"

358. Men who wear high heels and women who wear sneakers to the office

359. In high school, they were more likely to be in the audio-visual club than on the football team.

360. Anita Hill

361. Hillbilly Presidents

362. Hippies

☆☆☆☆☆☆☆☆☆☆☆☆☆☆☆☆☆☆☆☆

363.

364. Hipsters

365. Hip-Hop

366. They won't admit that they used to root for Ho Chi Minh.

367. They own more pairs of holey jeans than copies of the Holy Bible.

368. Hollywood producers

369. Hollywood fundraisers

370. Hollywood's PC values

371. The "homeless"

372. "Homeless" families being housed in what used to be first-class motels

373. Homeopathic medicine

374. "A place called Hope"

375. Hubert Horatio Humphrey

376. Willie Horton

377. They use "human rights" as an excuse to attack friendly anti-Communists.

378. They use humane traps for rats and mice so the vermin can breathe free in our backyards.

379. Their humorlessness

380. Hyannisport

381. Hyphenated Americans

382. Identity Politics

383. Lax immigration laws

384. "The nearest thing to immortality in this world is a government bureau."—General Hugh S. Johnson

☆☆☆☆☆☆☆☆☆☆☆☆☆☆☆☆☆☆☆☆☆☆☆☆

385. Incense

386. "Inclusiveness" as a code word for the exclusion of qualified straight white males

387. Inflation

388. Ingrates who can't get enough government handouts

389. Inner children who never stop whining

390. Inner children who would benefit from a good spanking

391. Their insufficient faith in technology

☆ ☆

392. Their insufficient respect for the flag

393. Investigative journalists

394. They would rather contribute to the Irish Republican Army than contribute to their own Individual Retirement Accounts.

395. The Iran hostage crisis

396. Ivy League Schools dominated by PC professors

397. Ivory-towered intellectuals who have never made (and could never make) a living in the real world

398. Jesse Jackson

399. Every jazz musician (except John Tesh)

400. Peter Jennings

401. "Thomas Jefferson founded the Democratic Party;
Franklin Roosevelt dumbfounded it."—Dewey Short

402. William Jefferson Clinton

403. They believe JFK was killed by the CIA and that Nicole
Brown Simpson was murdered by the LAPD

404. Job actions

☆ ☆

405. They have "jobs" rather than a career plan.

406. Clinton's jogs to McDonald's

407. Clinton's short jogging shorts and pasty white thighs

408. Paula Jones

409. They don't want to keep up with the Joneses. They'd rather drag the Joneses down to *their* level.

410. *The Joy of Sex* and other hedonist propaganda

411. Teddy Kennedy

412. William Kennedy Smith

413. They prefer the *Kinsey Report* to the Bible.

414. Kneejerk liberals

415. Mary Jo Kopechne

416. Maynard G. Krebs, who made bohemianism acceptable to a generation

417. William Kuntsler

418. Kwanzaa

419. Their laissez-faire attitude to home and lawn mainte-nance brings down all our property values.

420. Their Language Police have outlawed perfectly good descriptive words like "bum," "retard," "psycho," "hysteric," "spinster," and "cripple."

421. LBJ's scar

422. LBJ's son-in-law Chuck Robb, who kept a real patriot like Oliver North from sitting in the Senate.

423. LBJ's "war on poverty"

424. Lady Bird Johnson's war on billboards

425. "Its leaders are always troubadours of trouble; crooners of catastrophe . . . A Democratic president is doomed to proceed to his goals like a squid, squirting darkness all about him."—Clare Booth Luce

426. They learned their family values from *The Simpsons*.

427. They learned their history from Oliver Stone movies.

428. Leeches on the body politic

429. The New Left

430. The Old Left

☆☆☆☆☆☆☆☆☆☆☆☆☆☆☆☆☆☆☆☆☆☆☆☆

431. Legal Aid

432. The legalization of "recreational" drugs

433. The legalization of "victimless" crimes

434. Lemon laws and all other artificial restrictions on free automotive trade

435. Lenin

436. John Lennon

437. Lesbian chic

438. Prefer Letterman to Leno

439. Levis, the universal uniform of nonconformists

440. Liberals

441. "A liberal is a man who is willing to spend somebody else's money."—Carter Glass

442. They majored in Liberal Arts and are still upset because they haven't been able to find lucrative jobs as liberal artists.

443. Liberal guilt

444. The Liberal Media

445. "The liberals can understand everything but the people who don't understand them."—Lenny Bruce

446. Liberated women

447. "The Liberated Man"

448. Limousine liberals

449. Their lip service to middle class family values

450. When asked to list their liquid assets, they consider the semi-congealed dregs in their Jim Beam and Southern Comfort bottles.

451. Living in the past

452. Living in New York

453. Living in sin (but we repeat ourselves)

454. Logrolling ("I'll vote for your Neighborhood Abortion Center Act if you vote to fund my Robert Mapplethorpe exhibition.")

455. Longshoreman's unions

456. They refuse to take a long-term view of mergers, down-sizing, tax breaks, layoffs, and all other proactive efforts being made to enhance the competitiveness of American businesses (It's always "What about *my* job? *My* pension. *Me, Me, Me*").

457. The Loony Left

☆☆☆☆☆☆☆☆☆☆☆☆☆☆☆☆☆☆☆☆☆☆☆☆

458. Love-ins

459. The love that dare not speak its name

460. The love that used to dare not speak its name that now speaks its name over and over again

461. Low-fat Girl Scout cookies

462. Low-fat anything

463. Luddites

464. The lunatic fringe

465. Jimmy Carter's "lust in my heart"

466. They prefer Macintosh to Windows

467. Shirley MacLaine's current incarnation

468. Macrame

469. Macrobiotic diets of birdseed and water.

470. They made it impossible for us to sing the Flintstones theme song ("You'll have a gay old time!") without cringing.

471. The Madison Guaranty Savings and Loan

☆☆☆☆☆☆☆☆☆☆☆☆☆☆☆☆☆☆☆☆☆☆☆

472. They make great bartenders but lousy husbands.

473. Male high-school-homecoming queens

474. Malaise

475. They prefer Malcolm X to Malcolm Forbes.

476. Malt liquor

477. The delusion that Robert Mapplethorpe is an artist

478. They are more likely to have marched on Washington than in a military unit.

479. They prefer Herbert Marcuse to Neiman Marcus.

480.

481. They think "The Market" means the local Piggly Wiggly.

482. Martha Stewart-designed Christmas ornaments, from the Clinton White House

483. They still think Karl Marx was right "in theory."

484. Massachusetts, home of Ted Kennedy, Michael Dukakis, Barney Frank, and the only state to vote for George McGovern

485. George McGovern

486. George McGovern campaign veterans like Gary Hart and Bill Clinton

487. Men who ice skate but don't play hockey

488. Men who marry men

489. Mendacity

490. Military cutbacks

491. The Million Man March

492. Minnesota, home of Hubert Humphrey, socialist politics, and the only state to vote for Walter Mondale

493. They are more likely to have been in the vocal minority than the Silent Majority.

494. Miranda "Rights"

495. Jimmy Carter's Misery Index

496. Modern Architecture

☆ ☆

497. Mohawks (the hairstyle)

498. Walter "Fritz" Mondale

499. "The Democrats can't compete with the Republicans in spending money to get in office but after they get in I don't think there is anybody can compete with them."
—Will Rogers, 1920

500. They want money for nothing and their chicks for free.

501. The *Monkey Business*

502. Michael Moore (what's bad for GM is bad for the country)

503. Moral Relativism, or, "Who are we to give dietary advice to cannibals?"

504. Moratoriums

505. *Mother Jones*

506. Bill Moyers

507. *Ms.* (the magazine

508. Ms. (the appellation)

509. They encourage MTV viewers to "Rock the Vote."

☆☆☆☆☆☆☆☆☆☆☆☆☆☆☆☆☆☆☆☆☆☆☆☆

510. Muckrakers

511. Mudslinging

512. Multiculturalism

513. Multimedia classrooms that do not impinge on the self-esteem of the illiterate

514. They still refer to their hunger as "the munchies."

515. Edward R. Murrow

516. Ralph Nader

517. Naivete

518. The Nannygate troubles of Zoë Baird and Kimba Wood

519. They would rather name a whale after you than give you a real Christmas gift.

520. The Nation of Islam

521. The National Education Association

522. The National Endowment for the Arts

523. The National Endowment for the Humanities

☆☆☆☆☆☆☆☆☆☆☆☆☆☆☆☆☆☆☆☆☆☆☆

524. The National Institute of Occupational Safety and Health

525. The National Organization for Women

526. National Public Radio

527. The National Transportation Safety Board

528. "Nattering nabobs of negativism"

529. Neoliberals

530. They never met a tax they didn't pass

☆☆☆☆☆☆☆☆☆☆☆☆☆☆☆☆☆☆☆☆☆☆☆☆

531. New Age "music"

532. New Age "religion"

533. New Age anything

534. The New Covenant

535. The New Deal

536. The New Frontier

537. New York City

538. *The New Republic*

☆☆☆☆☆☆☆☆☆☆☆☆ ☆☆☆☆☆☆☆☆☆☆☆☆

☆☆☆☆☆☆☆☆☆☆☆☆☆☆☆☆☆☆☆☆☆☆☆☆

539. The *New York Times*

540. Hollywood's "nightmares of depravity" are their wet dreams.

541. They believe "the force" was with Luke Skywalker, but they didn't buy Ronald Reagan's Star Wars.

542. The 1930s

543. 1960

544. The 1960s

545. 1964

546. 1976

547. 1992

548. "No Nukes"

549. Jimmy Carter's shameless campaign for the Nobel Peace Prize

550. Noncompetitive "sports"

551. Nonconformists

552. Nonprofit organizations

553. Nonrepresentational art

554. NORML and other prodrug organizations

555. "Not inhaling"

556. Nude beaches

557. In your heart you know they're nuts.

558. They're offended by the names of traditional sports teams like the Indians, Chiefs, Braves, Redmen, and Redskins.

559. They prefer Om to Amen.

☆☆☆☆☆☆☆☆☆☆☆☆☆☆☆☆☆☆☆☆☆☆☆

560. One World Government

561. Open admission policies

562. Open Housing Laws

563. Open marriages

564. Operation PUSH

565. Oprah Winfrey's daily brainwashing of America's housewives

566. Organized Labor

567. Organized labor is just a front for organized crime

568. "I belong to no organized party—I am a Democrat."
—Will Rogers

569. OSHA

570. Outside agitators

571. PACs

572. Pacifists

573. Pagans

574. The (let's give away the) Panama Canal Treaty

575. Parasites

576. The parents who saddled their children with names like Moonbeam, River, Ocean, god, America, Flower, Dweezil, Psychedeliah, and Poohbear

577. "The first part of the Yippie program, you know, is kill your parents."—Jerry Rubin

578. Parlor Pinks

579. Pass-fail grading

☆☆☆☆☆☆☆☆☆☆☆☆☆☆☆☆☆☆☆☆☆☆☆☆

580. Patchouli

581. They *like* PBS fundraising marathons.

582.

583. Peanut farmers who insist on carrying their own bags
for the cameras when they disembark from Air Force One

☆☆☆☆☆☆☆☆☆☆☆☆☆☆☆☆☆☆☆☆☆☆☆

584. People for the American Way

585. People for the Ethical Treatment of Animals

586. Performance "artists"

587. Permissiveness

588. Their only hope in Presidential politics is H. Ross Perot's ability to split the Republican majority.

589. Peter, Paul and Mary

590. Peyote as a sacrament

☆ ☆

591. Phonetic spellings

592. Pierced ears on children

593. Pierced ears on men

594. Pierced noses or tongues or nipples or navels on anyone

595. Pierced body parts that people in polite society should only discuss with their urologists

596. The Pill

597. Pinkos

☆☆☆☆☆☆☆☆☆☆☆☆☆☆☆☆☆☆☆☆☆

598. Pious posturing about the poor

599. *Piss Christ*'s NEA subsidy

600. Planned Parenthood

601. Unplanned parenthood

602. Unwed parenthood

603. "Poetry" that doesn't rhyme

604. Poets

605. Policy wonks

☆☆☆☆☆☆☆☆☆☆☆☆☆☆☆☆☆☆☆☆☆☆

606. Political correctness

607. They see *Politically Correct Bedtime Stories* not as a parody, but as a long overdue public service.

608. They prefer pollution control to profits

609. Ponytails on men

610. Pork-barrel legislation

611. Pornography

612. The War on "Poverty"

613. They replaced prayer in schools with doctrinaire atheism.

614. They prefer spotted fruit to perfectly safe pesticides.

615. Premarital sex

616. Postmarital sex

617. Prey on the fears of the elderly

618. (The artist formerly known as) Prince

619. Prisoners' rights

620. They prefer Gibran's *The Prophet* to corporate profits.

☆ ☆

621. Progressive jazz

622. Progressive income taxes

623. Progressive anything

624. They prefer protesters to Protestants.

625. They have made it impossible for any upstanding heterosexual to send a postcard from Provincetown.

626. They are happy to see a psychiatrist unless it's suggested by their employer.

627. Public-access TV

☆☆☆☆☆☆☆☆☆☆☆☆☆☆☆☆☆☆☆☆☆☆☆☆

628. Public assistance

629. Public beaches

630. The Public Broadcasting System

631. Public defenders

632. Public financing of presidential elections

633. Public golf courses

634. Public Health Service

635. Public housing

☆ ☆

636. Public schools that we're forced to support with our property taxes even after we pay our $30,000-a-year tuition to Choate

637. Public sculpture of the sort Tom Wolfe called "The turd in the plaza"

638. Public transportation

639. Quakers

640. Quotas

641. Rabble rousers

☆☆☆☆☆☆☆☆☆☆☆☆☆☆☆☆☆☆☆☆☆☆☆

642. Radical Chic

643. The Rainbow Coalition

644. Rappers

645. They would still rather be Red than dead.

646. Dan Rather

647. Rebels without causes

648. Record company executives

649. Red ribbons

650. Red tape

651. The redesigned one hundred-dollar bill (They moved Franklin's portrait to the left and erased his politically-incorrect fur collar)

652. They refuse to accept a military rank lower than Commander-in-Chief.

653. Renault *Le Car*

654. Janet Reno

655. Reverse discrimination

656. *Revolution for the Hell of It*

☆☆☆☆☆☆☆☆☆☆☆☆☆☆☆☆☆☆☆☆☆☆

657. Donna Rice

658. Ann Richard's "Silver Foot" crack

659. Right-brain irrationality

660. They prefer the Right to Die to the Right to Life.

661. They want rights without responsibilities.

662. They romanticize the Rio Grande as America's new Ellis Island.

663. They refer to the 1992 L.A. riots as an "uprising."

664. Roach clips

665. The "Rodham" in Hillary Rodham Clinton

666. Roe *v.* Wade

667. Their "Rolexes" cost ten dollars and came from a suitcase.

668. The Rose Law Firm of Little Rock

669. They see the face of God in every homeless person and the face of Simon LeGree in the face of everyone who isn't.

670. Franklin Delano Roosevelt

671. Roseanne's gonad-grabbing disrespect for our national anthem

672. RU-486

673. Ruby Ridge

674. The Rust Belt

675. Saabs

676. "Safe" sex

677. Safety pins as jewelry

678. They prefer the free flow of salmon to cheap hydroelectric power.

679. "I never said all Democrats were saloonkeepers. What I said was that all saloonkeepers were Democrats."
—Will Rogers

680. They added "Saluting the Surgeon General" to the list of synonyms for sexual self-abuse.

681. Sandals

682. Sandinistas

☆☆☆☆☆☆☆☆☆☆☆☆☆☆☆☆☆☆☆☆☆☆☆☆

683. San Francisco

684. Susan Sarandon and Tim Robbins

685. They'd rather save the whales than save for their kid's education.

686. Clinton's saxophone (see reason number 40)

687. They prefer seances with Eleanor to tea with Nancy.

688. Seatbelt regulations

689. Seattle

☆☆☆☆☆☆☆☆☆☆☆☆☆☆☆☆☆☆☆☆☆☆☆☆

690. "A Sect or Party is . . . devised to save a man from the vexation of thinking."—Ralph Waldo Emerson

691. Secular humanism

692. The Securities and Exchange Commission

693. Self-righteousness

694. Sex acts requiring rubber suits and dental dams

695. Sex acts requiring more than two people

696. Sex acts requiring more than one person of the same gender

☆☆☆☆☆☆☆☆☆☆☆☆☆☆☆☆☆☆☆☆☆☆☆☆☆

697. Sex, Drugs, and Rock and Roll

698. Sex education is a requirement for high school graduation, but the ability to read a job application is not.

699. Shady Arkansas land deals

700. Their shortsighted opposition to clean, cheap, efficient atomic power

701. Sick day abuse

702. The "sick building" excuse

703. The Sierra Club

704. They prefer "significant others" to legal spouses.

705. The silence of the Eastern media establishment about Marilyn Monroe, Judith Exner, and the rest of JFK's playmates

706. Senator Paul Simon

707. Paul "'Rhymin'" Simon

708. They still can "roll their own."

709. They sleep in the nude

710. Single-prayer (yes, that means you) health plans

711. They learned to siphon gas in the Carter years.

712. Sit-ins

713. *60 Minutes* (except for Andy Rooney)

714. Slackers

715. Slick Willie

716. Girls' soccer

717. Social Diseases

☆ ☆

718. Social Engineering

719. Social Programs

720. Social Reform

721. They prefer Social Security to National Security.

722. Social workers who know better than parents what's best for America's children

723. Social Anything (other than the Social Register)

724. Socialism

☆☆☆☆☆☆☆☆☆☆☆☆☆☆☆☆☆☆☆☆☆☆☆☆

725. Socialized Medicine

726. Sociologists

727. Soy-based meat substitutes

728. They spare the rod.

729. In this era of special effects, they still expect us to believe that young Bill Clinton's handshake with JFK was more authentic than Forrest Gump's.

730. Special interests

731. Spin doctors

732. They prefer spotted owls to cheap lumber.

733. Spousal benefits for unmarried companions

734. They will give mouth-to-blowhole to a beached whale but won't allow a good steak to cross their lips.

735. Squatters

736. SSI checks for fakers

737. Stagflation

738. Lesley Stahl

739. They start long, drawn out wars like Korea and Vietnam rather than short snappy ones like Grenada, Panama, and Desert Storm.

740. Statehood for D.C.

741. Statehood for Puerto Rico

742. Gloria Steinem

743. George Stephanopoulos

744. Thanks to them, we'll never see Stimey on TV again

745. Michael "Meathead" Stivic

746. Barbra Streisand

747. Students for a Democratic Society

748. They prefer subcultures to culture.

749. They prefer swamps to subdivisions.

750. Tammany Hall

751. Tattoos

752. Tax-and-spend

753. Teachers who show sixth graders how to put condoms on bananas

754. They recognize the smell of tear gas

755. 1040 forms

756. They think golf is just a game.

757. They think the government owes them a living.

758. They think that after death they will "go to the light" instead of straight to hell.

759. Third World romanticism

☆ ☆

760. They prefer McGovern's "1,000 percent support" to Bush's "thousand points of light."

761. They laugh *with* the Three Stooges, not *at* them.

762. They throw our money at their problems.

763. They prefer Thunderbird, the "wine," to the car.

764. Laws that tie the hands of the police

765. Tie-dyed anything

766. Clinton's tacky plastic Timex Ironman watch

☆☆☆☆☆☆☆☆☆☆☆☆☆☆☆☆☆☆☆☆☆☆☆☆

767. Tofu

768. The token liberals on *The McLaughlin Group*

769. Toll roads that subsidize mass transit

770. Female toplessness as an equal-rights issue

771. Nina Totenberg

772. Trailer parks

773. Traitors

774. Trampling on States' Rights

☆☆☆☆☆☆☆☆☆☆☆☆☆☆☆☆☆☆☆☆☆☆☆

775. Transactional Analysis

776. Transcendental Meditation

777. Transsexuals

778. Transvestites

779. Travelgate

780. Tree hugging

781. Tree-spiking terrorists

782. Trendy curriculum like "deconstruction"

☆☆☆☆☆☆☆☆☆☆☆☆☆☆☆☆☆☆☆☆☆☆☆

783. Troopergate

784. Troublemakers

785. They trust government more than business

786. Trust-funded radicals

787. Boss Tweed

788. They tie the hands of honest businessmen with bureaucratic red tape.

789. Underachievers

☆☆☆☆☆☆☆☆☆☆☆☆☆☆☆☆☆☆☆☆☆☆☆☆☆

790. The underclass

791. "Underground" movies

792. "Underground" newspapers

793. They understand that "boys will be boys" when it's the Kennedys but not when it's the Tailhook Association.

794. Clinton's "underwear" press conference on MTV

795. Unemployment compensation

796. Unemployment insurance

797. UNESCO

798. They favored unilateral nuclear disarmament in the 1980s.

799. Unions

800. Union Halls and other excuses to drink

801. Unisex hairstyles

802. Unisex clothing

803. Unisex perfume

☆☆☆☆☆☆☆☆☆☆☆☆☆☆☆☆☆☆☆☆☆☆☆

804. Unitarians

805. The United Auto Workers

806. The United Farm Workers

807. The United Mine Workers

808. The United Nations

809. Unsolicited windshield cleanings

810. Upper West Side

811. They used to be Communists.

☆☆☆☆☆☆☆☆☆☆☆☆☆☆☆☆☆☆☆☆☆☆☆☆

812. They're usually richer than they look.

813. Naive utopianism

814. Their idea of an effective anti-vagrancy law is to make a
calling a vagrant "a vagrant" a hate crime.

815. Vegans

816. Vegetarians

817. Veggie-burgers

818. They don't consider venereal disease to be a sin, or a
politically correct designation.

819. Vermont, home of Ben and Jerry's, "back to nature" hippies, and the country's only socialist congressman.

820. They have a vested interest in preserving a large intact underclass.

821. Victims

822. The draft dodger in the White House officially recognized Communist Vietnam.

823. The Village People

824. the village VOICE

825. Didn't learn *that* vocabulary from William F. Buckley

826. To you, it's a 1977 Volaré up on blocks; to them, it's lawn sculpture.

827. Volkswagen bugs that block your Lexus on the highway

828. Volvos with "You Can't Hug With Nuclear Arms" bumper stickers

829. The Voting Rights Act

830. Aggressive voter registration drives aimed at signing up the poor, the uneducated, and the non-English-speaking

831. The vulgarization of American culture

832. Waco

833. Wackos

834. Waffling

835. Waitrons and chairpersons

836. Lawrence Walsh and his Iran-Contra revelations on the eve of the '92 election

837. Ward healers

838. The Warren Court

839. Washable silk

840. They would rather teach kids about George Washington Carver than George Washington.

841. Washington, D.C.

842. *The Washington Post*

843. Weasel words

844. The Weathermen (and we don't mean Willard and Al Roker)

☆ ☆

845. Welfare

846. Welfare mothers

847. Wetbacks

848. Using Wetlands legislation to halt all development

849. When they're not groping someone else's wife, they're groping your wallet.

850. Whiners

851. Whistle blowers

852. White-man bashing

853. Whitewater

☆☆☆☆☆☆☆☆☆☆☆☆☆☆☆☆☆☆☆☆☆☆☆☆☆

854. Whole Language (hoo carze if eye kan spel?)

855. WIC giveaways

856. "Windfall" profits taxes

857. Federally mandated women's sports (other than field hockey and cheerleading)

858. Women's Studies

859. Women's Suffrage

860. Women who refuse to shave their legs and armpits

861. Women who wear the pants in the family

862. Women who wear pants

863. Women who don't get married

864. Women who "marry" women

865. Women who marry men, but keep their maiden names

866. Women who insist on using their maiden name as their middle name (only excusable if you are trying to distance yourself from a husband named Clinton)

867. Women who get married, take their husband's name, but don't have children

868. Women who have children but don't get married and expect the rest of us to pick up the tab for their little bastards

869. Women

☆☆☆☆☆☆☆☆☆☆☆☆☆☆☆☆☆☆☆☆☆☆☆☆☆

870. Womyn who are linguistically offended by the "man" in "woman" and the "son" in "person."

871. They won't go to the bathroom without a government safety net.

872.

873. Woodstock II

874. Woodward and Bernstein

875. Workers

876. Worker's compensation laws

877. They prefer work force diversity to work force productivity.

878. Working-class wannabes

879. They worry about Flipper every time they open a can of Chicken of the Sea.

880. The wrong side of the tracks

881. "X" baseball caps

882. Yard sales

☆ ☆

883. Yippies

884. Yoga

885. Yogurt as a substitute for the three-martini lunch

886. Yugos

887. They prefer zircons to good old-fashioned South African diamonds.

888. ZPG (zero population growth, and the number of miles they want you to get per gallon)